Italy

by Sarah E. De Capua

Content Adviser: Roger Pirrone,
Italidea, Chicago, Illinois

Reading Adviser: Dr. Linda D. Labbo,
Department of Reading Education, College of Education,
The University of Georgia

COMPASS POINT BOOKS

Minneapolis, Minnesota

FIRST REPORTS

Compass Point Books
3109 West 50th Street, #115
Minneapolis, MN 55410

Visit Compass Point Books on the Internet at *www.compasspointbooks.com*
or e-mail your request to *custserv@compasspointbooks.com*

Cover: Fountain and Spanish steps in Rome

Photographs©: Dennis Degnan/Corbis, cover; Charles McRue/Visuals Unlimited, 4; John Elk III, 6–7, 23, 27; Photo Network/Chad Ehlers, 8–9, 22; John and Lisa Merrill/Corbis, 10; Mark L. Stephenson/Corbis, 11; Photo Network/Paul Thompson, 12, 42–43; Maurizio Lanini/Corbis, 13; Scala/Art Resource, N.Y., 15, 16–17; Giraudon/Art Resource, N.Y., 18; Corbis, 19; Hulton-Deutsch Collection/Corbis, 20; Nicolas Sapieha/Corbis, 21; Stephanie Maze/Corbis, 24; Richard Hamilton Smith/Corbis, 25; Dennis Marsico/ Corbis, 26; Sergio Pitamitz/Corbis, 28–29; David Lees/Corbis, 30; PhotoDisc, 31, 36, 41; Jim Yokajty/The Image Finders, 32, 40; Courtesy arezzoweb.com, 33; Hulton/Archive by Getty Images, 34, 35; Owen Franken/Corbis, 37; Bob Krist/Corbis, 38; Bill Ross/Corbis, 39.

Editors: E. Russell Primm, Emily J. Dolbear, and Patricia Stockland
Photo Researcher: Svetlana Zhurkina
Photo Selector: Linda S. Koutris
Designer/Page Production: Bradfordesign, Inc./Biner Design
Cartographer: XNR Productions, Inc.

Library of Congress Cataloging-in-Publication Data
De Capua, Sarah.
   Italy / by Sarah De Capua.
      p. cm. — (First reports)
  Summary: Introduces the geography, history, culture, and people of Italy, the boot-shaped country in southern Europe. Includes bibliographical references and index.
   ISBN 0-7565-0426-0 (hardcover)
   1. Italy—Juvenile literature. [1. Italy.] I. Title. II. Series
   DG417 .D4 2003
945—dc21
                                     2002009927

Table of Contents

"Ciao!" 4

Land and Weather 8

Italy's History 14

Made in Italy 22

Life in Italy 24

Festivals and Holidays 28

Arts and Literature 31

Italian Food 36

Rome—The Capital 39

Italy Today 42

Glossary 44

Did You Know? 44

At a Glance 45

Important Dates 46

Want to Know More? 47

Index 48

*NOTE: In this book, words that are defined in the glossary are in **bold** the first time they appear in the text.*

"Ciao!"

▲ *The Sicilian city of Taromina*

Can you say "*ciao*" (CHOW)? You have just said hello
in Italian! It can also mean good-bye.

Italy is a country in Europe. It is shaped like a
boot. Italy is a **peninsula.** It juts out into the ocean.

The island at the toe of Italy's boot is Sicily. It is part of Italy. The island to the west of Italy is Sardinia. It is part of Italy, too.

▲ *Map of Italy*

Italy touches four countries. France lies northwest of Italy. Switzerland is north of Italy. Austria and Slovenia are northeast of Italy.

Five seas surround Italy and its islands. The Ligurian and Tyrrhenian Seas extend along Italy's west coast. The Ionian Sea lies to Italy's south. The Adriatic Sea borders Italy on the east. The Mediterranean Sea touches Sardinia and Sicily.

Italy is known for its old buildings, beautiful works of art, and delicious food. Many people visit Italy every year. More than 57 million people call it home.

Rome is the capital of Italy. It is also the country's largest city. Other major cities are Turin, Venice, Milan, and Naples.

▲ *Tourists visit the Roman Forum, where the government of ancient Rome was centered.*

Land and Weather

Italy has a lot of mountains. The Alps cover the north. Mont Blanc is here. It reaches 15,771 feet (4,810 meters) into the sky. Mont Blanc is the highest mountain in Italy. Monte Cervino, also called the Matterhorn, is on the border between Italy and Switzerland. Many people have climbed this steep peak. A mountain range called the Apennines rises from central Italy.

Some of the mountains in Italy are volcanoes. Lava, ash, rock, steam, and gas have come out of these volcanoes in the past. Mount Etna is on the island of Sicily. It is

▲ *A view of the Alps and the town of Cortina d'Ampezzo*

Europe's tallest volcano. Mount Vesuvius is a volcano near Naples. In A.D. 79, Vesuvius erupted. The cities of Pompeii and Herculaneum were buried under mud, ash, and rock.

▲ *Mount Vesuvius towering over the ruins of Pompeii*

▲ *The Tiber River flows through Rome.*

The Po Valley is in the northern part of the country. The Po River is Italy's longest river. It flows through the Po Valley. The land here is good for farming. Other major rivers in Italy include the Arno, the Tiber, and the Volturno.

Long ago, **glaciers** carved out part of the land in northern Italy. These areas later filled with water. Now they are large lakes. They include Maggiore, Lugano, Como, and Garda.

Italy's weather varies. In the Alps, winters are long and cold. There is a lot of snowfall. Summers are short

◄ This painted vase shows the talent of an ancient Etruscan artist.

In 49 B.C., Julius Caesar became the ruler. He created an **empire.** Caesar's powerful Roman Empire covered much of Europe. Caesar was murdered on March 15, 44 B.C. His great-nephew, Augustus, became emperor in 29 B.C. For the next 200 years, the people of the empire lived in peace.

In A.D. 476, the last emperor of ancient Rome was overthrown. After the fall of Rome, different leaders ruled. In the year 800, the pope chose Charlemagne as the new emperor of the Romans. Charlemagne solved many problems, but his empire ended after his death in 814.

Around the year 1000, Italy was made up of **city-states.** The arts and sciences grew during a time called the Renaissance, which began in the 1300s. In the 1400s, other European nations began to attack Italy. The French came first, followed by the Spanish. Later, Austria ruled northern Italy.

▲ *This painting by Italian artist Vincenzo Camuccini shows the death of Julius Caesar.*

Napoléon named himself king of Italy.

From 1796 to 1814, the French returned. Napoléon Bonaparte led the French. He took over Italy and named himself king.

Tired of foreign rule, Italians fought three wars of independence from 1848 to 1861. Giuseppe Garibaldi, a famous Italian hero, organized 1,000 men to free southern Italy. In 1861, King Vittorio Emanuele announced the creation of the kingdom of Italy. This new kingdom experienced many problems, including debt, after fighting the wars. Also, the people of the north and south were very different.

◄ *Giuseppe Garibaldi was a hero to the Italian people.*

European allies Benito Mussolini (left) and Adolf Hitler of Germany

The Italian kingdom lasted until after World War I (1914–1918). In 1922, Benito Mussolini used force to take power as prime minister. He sided with Germany during World War II (1939–1945) and was defeated in the war. In 1945, Mussolini was killed by his own people. Italy became an independent republic in 1946.

Today, Italy's government is made up of a **parliament.** The parliament has a Chamber of Deputies and a Senate. Members of parliament are elected by the people. Parliament members elect a president. The president chooses a prime minister. Both of these leaders work with parliament to run the country.

▲ *The interior of the Italian parliament in Rome*

Made in Italy

Italy sells many things to other countries such as food, drinks, clothing, and cars. Favorite Italian foods and

drinks include pasta, tomatoes, olives, anchovies, and wines. Italy is the world's leading wine maker. It is second only to Spain in the production of olive oil.

Italian fashion is famous. People come from all over the world to see the new fashions from Italian designers. Milan is Italy's fashion center.

▲ Grapes are harvested in Greve to make wine.

▲ *A car show in Padua*

The most famous Italian car is the Ferrari. Other well-known cars made in Italy are the Fiat, the Lamborghini, and the Maserati. Car factories are in northern Italy.

Italian factories produce iron, steel, and chemicals. Other factories bottle, can, and preserve fruits and vegetables.

Life in Italy

Family life is very important in Italy. Parents, grandparents, children, and sometimes aunts and uncles all live together in the same home. Most families live in or near cities. They live in apartment buildings or houses. Italian families spend a lot of time together, especially at meals.

Children must go to school from the age of six to fourteen.

◀ A family in Sulmona comes together for dinner.

Some children as young as three years old attend kindergarten. Most Italian children attend public schools. Some go to private schools run by the Catholic Church.

The school year runs from September to June. The school day begins at 8:30 A.M. It ends at 1:30 P.M. twice a week and at 4 P.M. three times a week. Children go home to eat lunch. Many play sports such as soccer, volleyball, and basketball.

Italians relax by going for walks and gathering at the town square. People also meet at outdoor cafés and restaurants.

▲ *Children playing soccer in Pisa*

Would you like to go on vacation for an entire month? Then Italy may be the place for you. Many Italians vacation for the entire month of August. Some like to go to the mountains. Others prefer a vacation at the beach.

Soccer is the favorite sport to play and to watch in Italy. Cycling and Formula One car racing are also popular. Italians enjoy other sports such as tennis, fishing, and skiing.

▲ *A mountain bike race near Siena*

Most people in Italy are Roman Catholics. They worship in the many beautiful churches and cathedrals throughout the country. Some of these churches have existed for hundreds of years. They are filled with paintings and other art that show people and scenes from the Bible.

◀ *Siena Cathedral in Tuscany is one of many Roman Catholic churches in Italy.*

Festivals and Holidays

Italians take pleasure in many holidays and festivals. Venice puts on an international film festival every year. Festivals of Unity, with concerts, dances, and art shows, are held throughout Italy. Before **Lent,** people hold carnivals. Many Italians and visitors go to the Viareggio Carnival and the Venice Carnival. People wear colorful costumes and masks and ride on parade floats.

Italians also enjoy good food, and they have many festivals to celebrate it. People from towns where grapes grow often celebrate the end of the grape season.

Do you like spaghetti? Then you might want to visit the town of Torre Annunziata. The Festival of Spaghetti is held there.

▲ *The Venice Carnival is famous for its many interesting costumes.*

Important holidays in Italy include New Year's Day (January 1), Liberation Day (April 25), and Labor Day (May 1). Religious holidays are especially important because they celebrate events in the Catholic religion. These holidays include Christmas, the Befana (January 6), Easter, and the Feast of the Immaculate Conception (December 8).

▲ Bagpipers playing Christmas tunes in Rome

Arts and Literature

▲ *This famous sculpture of Moses by Italian artist Michelangelo is located in Rome.*

Art has always been a part of the Italian culture. Italians have painted some of the world's most famous paintings. Museums and churches, as well as Vatican Palace, display many great works of art. Artist Leonardo da Vinci painted *The Last Supper*, which is a scene of Jesus Christ's last meal with his followers. Botticelli, Michelangelo, and Titian are other famous Italian artists.

Architecture is the art of designing and building structures. Italian-style architecture is famous throughout the world. The Colosseum in Rome was built during the days of the Roman Empire. It was completed around A.D. 80.

Many cathedrals in Italy are world famous. St. Peter's Basilica in Rome is one of the largest buildings in the

▲ *A view inside the Roman Colosseum*

world. Another famous example is the Duomo of Orvieto. In modern times, Rome's Palazzeto dello Sport stadium and Milan's Pirelli skyscraper are important buildings.

Many Italians love music. Italian composers, musicians, and instruments have given the world great music. In the 500s, the Catholic Church created Gregorian chant. About 500 years later, a system for writing down music was invented by a monk named Guido d'Arezzo. Did you know that the violin, cello, and piano were all created in Italy?

▲ A statue of Guido d'Arezzo in Arezzo

Opera and orchestra music began in the 1600s. Sonatas are musical pieces usually played by one or two instruments. Sonatas were first played in Italy in the 1700s.

Italians enjoy operas, which tell stories with music and singers. Italians wrote many of the world's most famous operas, including *Aida*, *The Barber of Seville*, and *Madame Butterfly*. Two of the best-known Italian opera composers are Giacomo Puccini and Giuseppe Verdi. Luciano Pavarotti is a world-famous Italian opera singer.

▲ *Italian composer Giacomo Puccini in the early 1900s*

One of Italy's greatest works of literature is *The Divine Comedy*. Dante Alighieri wrote this long poem in the early 1300s. Another writer from that time was Giovanni Boccaccio, who is known for his short stories. Luigi Pirandello wrote more modern plays. In 1934, he received the Nobel Prize for Literature. You may know *The Adventures of Pinocchio*—the famous story about a puppet that comes to life. It was written by an Italian named Carlo Collodi in 1883.

◀ *Famous Italian playwright Luigi Pirandello in 1929*

Italian Food

▲ *Cappuccino is a famous Italian coffee drink popular all over the world.*

Italians love food. Pizza, pasta, cannoli, and cappuccino all come from Italy. The country is known for its parmesan, gorgonzola, and mozzarella cheeses.

The main meal is eaten at midday or in the evening. Often, a plate of antipasto is served at the beginning of a meal. Bread and olive oil, meats such

as salami and prosciutto, and cheese might be included. Minestrone is a popular thick vegetable soup. Many Italian meals include pasta or risotto. Pasta is often served with tomato or other flavorful sauce. Risotto is a rice dish from northern Italy. Meat or vegetable dishes may also be served.

◄ *This pasta is served with clams and broccoli.*

Many delicious desserts come from Italy. Cannoli is one popular kind of pastry. Zuppa inglese is a popular cake. If you like ice cream, sample some gelato. That is Italian ice cream.

Almost all Italian meals include some kind of fresh bread and wine. Many different kinds of wine are enjoyed throughout Italy.

◀ *Gelato at a café in Pizzo*

▲ *In Venice, boats called gondolas are used to travel on the city's many canals.*

Glossary

artifacts—objects made by humans, especially tools or weapons used in the past

city-states—areas that have their own laws and are each made up of a city and the surrounding territory

empire—a group of countries under one ruler or government, with one country having control over the rest

glaciers—huge sheets of ice that move slowly over land

Lent—the forty days before Easter, not including Sundays, usually honored by Christians as a time for prayer and serious thought

parliament—a group of people who are elected to make laws

peninsula—a piece of land that sticks out from a larger landmass and is almost completely surrounded by water

republic—a form of government in which the people elect representatives to manage the government

Did You Know?

- The ruins of Pompeii and Herculaneum have been uncovered. Visitors can see what life was like in these ancient Roman towns nearly 2,000 years ago.

- The ancient Romans gave Italy its name. They called the southern peninsula *Italia*, meaning "land of oxen."

- The Vatican isn't the only separate city-state in Italy. San Marino is in northeastern Italy. It is like a country within a country.

- The Italian flag is called the *Tricolore,* or "three colors."

At a Glance

Official name: Republic of Italy

Capital: Rome

Official language: Italian

National song: "L'Inno di Mameli" ("Hymn of Mameli")

Area: 116,341 square miles (301,323 square kilometers)

Highest point: Mont Blanc at 15,771 feet (4,810 meters)

Lowest point: Mediterranean Sea at sea level

Population: 57,715,625 (2002 estimate)

Head of government: Prime minister

Money: Euro

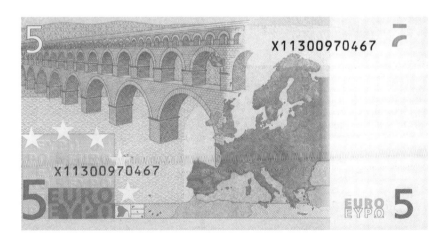

Important Dates

4000 B.C.	Hunters cross the Alps and move into what is now Italy.
800 B.C.	Etruscans establish a culture in Italy.
510 B.C.	Etruscan rule ends, and an Italian republic is set up.
49 B.C.	Julius Caesar establishes the Roman Empire. Five years later, he is murdered.
29 B.C.	Augustus becomes emperor.
A.D. 476	The last Roman emperor is overthrown.
800	Charlemagne becomes emperor and dies fourteen years later.
1000	City-states in Italy become more important.
1796	Napoléon Bonaparte takes over Italy.
1814	Napoléon's rule ends.
1861	After three wars of independence, the kingdom of Italy is created.
1922	Benito Mussolini uses force to become prime minister.
1945	Mussolini is killed by his own people.
1946	Italy becomes an independent republic.
2001	The euro replaces the lira as Italy's currency.

Want to Know More?

At the Library

Nickles, Greg. *Italy: The Culture.* New York: Crabtree, 2001.

Peterson, David. *Italy.* Danbury, Conn.: Children's Press, 2001.

Stroud, Jonathan. *Ancient Rome: A Guide to the Glory of Imperial Rome.* New York: Larousse Kingfisher Chambers, 2000.

On the Web

Italy

http://www.italyemb.org

For traveling tips, Italian activities in the United States, and news

Let's Roam Italy

http://www.thinkquest.org/library.html

For information about the culture of the major Italian cities, the Roman Empire, and the Italian Renaissance

Pompeii

http://www.pompeii.co.uk

For a description of the discoveries at Pompeii, color photos, maps, and virtual tours

Through the Mail

Embassy of Italy in the United States

3000 Whitehaven Street, N.W.

Washington, DC 20008

202/612-4400

To learn more about Italy and to plan a trip

On the Road

Upstate New York Italian Cultural Center and Museum

668 Catherine Street

Utica, NY 13501

To learn more about Italy and Italian immigrants

Index

Alps, 8, 12
architecture, 32–33
art, 31
automobile industry, 23
Bonaparte, Napoléon, 18
Caesar, Augustus, 16
Caesar, Julius, 16
Charlemagne (emperor), 16
children, 24–25
Colosseum, 32
cycling, 26
Duomo of Orvieto, 33
farming, 11
fashion industry, 22
festivals, 28
foods, 22, 28–29, 36–38
Formula One car racing, 26
government, 14, 16, 17–21, 39
holidays, 28, 30
housing, 24
lakes, 12
language, 4
Leaning Tower, 42
Matterhorn, 8
Milan, 6, 22, 33

mountains, 8, 10
music, 33–34
Mussolini, Benito, 20
parliament, 20–21
Pavarotti, Luciano, 34
Pompeii, 10
religion, 25, 27, 30, 33, 41
Renaissance, 17
rivers, 11
Roman Empire, 16, 32, 40
Rome, 6, 16, 32, 33, 39–41, 42
Sardinia, 5, 6
schools, 24–25
sports, 25, 26, 33
St. Peter's Basilica, 32–33
Tiber River, 11, 39
tourism, 6, 42
vacations, 26
Vatican, 41
Venice, 6, 28, 42
Vinci, Leonardo da, 31
volcanoes, 8, 10
weather, 12–13
World War I, 20
World War II, 20

About the Author

Sarah E. De Capua's Italian ancestors came from Sicily and the town of Capua, northeast of Naples. Capua contains ruins of a coliseum that is a hundred years older than Rome's Colosseum! When she is not researching her family tree, De Capua works as an author and editor of children's books. She lives in Colorado.